I0838983

THE NEWS IN 52 QUOTES

THE NEWS IN 52 QUOTES

KIT

LESS IS MORE

Ludwig Mies van der Rohe

INTRODUCTION

The News has always worn two hats.   It's been seen simultaneously as a revealer of the truth, and perpetrator of lies; protector of democracy, and killer of culture; a check on the powerful and a tool of entrenched power.

For their part, journalists are first responders to injustice at their best. At their worst, well, see the words of Hunter S. Thompson in these pages.

The News in 52 Quotes is a concise collection of wisdom telling us what the news is, what it can be, where it fails, and how it can succeed.

- Kit

"WE DON'T GO INTO JOURNALISM TO BE POPULAR. IT IS OUR JOB TO SEEK THE TRUTH AND PUT CONSTANT PRESSURE ON OUR LEADERS UNTIL WE GET ANSWERS."

— HELEN THOMAS

"THE PEOPLE MUST KNOW BEFORE THEY CAN ACT, AND THERE IS NO EDUCATOR TO COMPARE WITH THE PRESS."

— IDA B. WELLS
SOUTHERN HORRORS

"IF YOU AREN'T CAREFUL, THE NEWSPAPERS WILL HAVE YOU HATING THE PEOPLE WHO ARE BEING OPPRESSED AND LOVING THE PEOPLE WHO ARE DOING THE OPPRESSING."

— MALCOLM X

"I STILL BELIEVE THAT IF YOUR AIM IS TO CHANGE THE WORLD, JOURNALISM IS A MORE IMMEDIATE SHORT-TERM WEAPON."

— TOM STOPPARD

"THE QUEST OF THE TRUTH HAD BEEN BORN IN ME - THE MOST TRAGIC AND INCOMPLETE, AS WELL AS THE MOST ESSENTIAL, OF MAN'S QUESTS."

— IDA TARBELL

"WHATEVER A PATRON DESIRES TO GET PUBLISHED IS ADVERTISING; WHATEVER HE WANTS TO KEEP OUT OF THE PAPER IS NEWS."

— ANONYMOUS

"IF JOURNALISM IS GOOD, IT IS CONTROVERSIAL, BY ITS NATURE."

— JULIAN ASSANGE

"WHEN YOU CONTROL OPINION, AS CORPORATE AMERICA CONTROLS OPINION IN THE UNITED STATES BY OWNING THE MEDIA, YOU CAN MAKE THE MASSES BELIEVE ALMOST ANYTHING YOU WANT, AND GUIDE THEM AS YOU PLEASE."

— GORE VIDAL

"JOURNALISM IS ONE OF THE DEVICES WHEREBY INDUSTRIAL AUTOCRACY KEEPS ITS CONTROL OVER POLITICAL DEMOCRACY; IT IS THE DAY-BY-DAY, BETWEEN-ELECTIONS PROPAGANDA, WHEREBY THE MINDS OF THE PEOPLE ARE KEPT IN A STATE OF ACQUIESCENCE, SO THAT WHEN THE CRISIS OF AN ELECTION COMES, THEY GO TO THE POLLS AND CAST THEIR BALLOTS FOR EITHER ONE OF THE TWO CANDIDATES OF THEIR EXPLOITERS."

— UPTON SINCLAIR

"WE WANT YOU TO LOVE US OR HATE US. WE JUST DON'T WANT YOU TO BE INDIFFERENT."

— SHANE SMITH

"EXPRESSING OPINIONS THAT ARE IN ACCORD WITH, AND WHICH SERVE THE INTERESTS OF, THOSE WHO WIELD THE GREATEST POLITICAL AND ECONOMIC POWER IS ALWAYS ACCEPTABLE FOR THE JOURNALISTS WHO MOST TIGHTLY EMBRACE THE PRETENSE OF 'NEUTRALITY'; IT'S ONLY WHEN AN OPINION CONSTITUTES DISSENT OR WHEN IT'S EXPRESSED WITH TO LITTLE REVERENCE FOR THE MOST POWERFUL DOES IT CROSS THE LINE INTO 'ACTIVISM' AND 'BIAS.'"

— JACK SCHAFER

"I DON'T BELIEVE NEWSPAPER REPORTERS CAN SUBSTITUTE FOR A DISTRICT ATTORNEY, BUT A NEWSPAPER HAS A VERY VALID INVESTIGATIVE ROLE. NEWSPAPER REPORTS ON CORRUPTION IN GOVERNMENT, RACKETEERING AND ORGANIZED CRIME CONDITIONS CAN BE VERY HELPFUL TO YOUR COMMUNITIES AND THE WHOLE COUNTRY."

— ROBERT KENNEDY

"THE JOURNALIST MUST STRIVE TO FIND OUT WHAT IS GOING ON AND TELL IT, NOT NEUTER THE TRUTH IN THE NAME OF EQUAL TIME."

— JOE SACCO

JOURNALISM

"AS A YOUNG JOURNALIST, I THOUGHT THAT STORIES WERE SIMPLY WHAT HAPPENED. AS A SCREENWRITER, I REALIZED THAT WE *CREATE* STORIES BY IMPOSING NARRATIVE ON THE EVENTS THAT HAPPEN AROUND US."

— NORA EPHRON

"REMEMBER THAT THE MEDIA HAVE TWO BASIC FUNCTIONS. ONE IS TO INDOCTRINATE THE ELITES, TO MAKE SURE THEY HAVE THE RIGHT IDEAS AND KNOW HOW TO SERVE POWER. IN FACT, TYPICALLY THE ELITES ARE THE MOST INDOCTRINATED SEGMENT OF A SOCIETY, BECAUSE THEY ARE THE ONES WHO ARE EXPOSED TO THE MOST PROPAGANDA AND ACTUALLY TAKE PART IN THE DECISION-MAKING PROCESS. FOR THEM YOU HAVE THE NEW YORK TIMES, AND THE WASHINGTON POST, AND THE WALL STREET JOURNAL, AND SO ON. BUT THERE'S ALSO A MASS MEDIA, WHOSE MAIN FUNCTION IS JUST TO GET RID OF THE REST OF THE POPULATION—TO MARGINALIZE AND ELIMINATE THEM, SO THEY DON'T INTERFERE WITH DECISION-MAKING. AND THE PRESS THAT'S DESIGNED FOR THAT PURPOSE ISN'T THE NEW YORK TIMES AND THE WASHINGTON POST, IT'S SITCOMS ON TELEVISION, AND THE NATIONAL ENQUIRER, AND SEX AND VIOLENCE, AND BABIES WITH THREE HEADS, AND FOOTBALL, ALL THAT KIND OF STUFF."

— NOAM CHOMSKY

"PERHAPS THE BIGGEST PROBLEM IN JOURNALISM IS THE CULT DIVIDE BETWEEN JOURNALISTS AND CORPORATE OWNERS."

— KEN AULETTA

"THE PRESS, WATSON, IS A MOST VALUABLE INSTITUTION, IF YOU ONLY KNOW HOW TO USE IT."

— ARTHUR CONAN DOYLE

THE SIX NAPOLEONS

"HOW DO YOU STAND UP TO A DICTATOR? "BY EMBRACING VALUES DEFINED EARLY. HONESTY, VULNERABILITY, EMPATHY, MOVING AWAY FROM EMOTIONS, EMBRACING YOUR FEAR, BELIEVING IN THE GOOD. YOU CAN'T DO IT ALONE. YOU HAVE TO CREATE A TEAM, STRENGTHEN YOUR AREA OF INFLUENCE, THEN CONNECT THE BRIGHT SPOTS AND WEAVE THE MESH TOGETHER. AVOID THINKING IN TERMS OF US AGAINST THEM. STAND IN SOMEONE ELSE'S SHOES AND DO UNTO OTHERS AS YOU WOULD HAVE THEM DO UNTO YOU. TECHNOLOGY HAS PROVEN THAT HUMAN BEINGS HAVE FAR MORE IN COMMON THAN WE HAVE DIFFERENCES."

— MARIA RESSA
HOW TO STAND UP TO A DICTATOR

"HITLER HAS WRITTEN IN HIS BOOK THAT YOU CAN GET ANY LIE BELIEVED IF YOU REPEAT IT OFTEN ENOUGH; AND ESPECIALLY IF IT'S A BIG LIE— BECAUSE PEOPLE WILL SAY THAT NOBODY WOULD DARE TO TELL ONE AS BIG AS THAT."

— UPTON SINCLAIR
WIDE IS THE GATE

"RAGE IS THE ONLY QUALITY WHICH HAS KEPT ME, OR ANYBODY I HAVE EVER STUDIED, WRITING COLUMNS FOR NEWSPAPERS."

— JIMMY BRESLIN

"JOURNALISM WITHOUT A MORAL POSITION IS IMPOSSIBLE. EVERY JOURNALIST IS A MORALIST. IT'S ABSOLUTELY UNAVOIDABLE."

— MARGUERITE DURAS

"BUT SOMETHING VERY BAD HAPPENED TO THE NEWS MEDIA IN THE 1980S. PART OF IT WAS THE 'PUBLIC DIPLOMACY' PRESSURES FROM THE OUTSIDE. BUT PART OF IT WAS THE SMUG, SNOTTY, SOPHOMORIC CROWD THAT CAME TO DOMINATE THE NATIONAL MEDIA FROM THE INSIDE. THESE CHARACTERS FELL IN LOVE WITH THEIR POWER TO DEFINE REALITY, NOT THEIR RESPONSIBILITY TO UNCOVER THE FACTS. BY THE 1990S, THE MEDIA HAD BECOME THE MONSTER."

— GARY WEBB
DARK ALLIANCE

"AS FAR AS I'M CONCERNED, IT'S A DAMNED SHAME THAT A FIELD AS POTENTIALLY DYNAMIC AND VITAL AS JOURNALISM SHOULD BE OVERRUN WITH DULLARDS, BUMS, AND HACKS, HAG-RIDDEN WITH MYOPIA, APATHY, AND COMPLACENCE, AND GENERALLY STUCK IN A BOG OF STAGNANT MEDIOCRITY."

— HUNTER S. THOMPSON

"DON'T WORRY ABOUT TALKING TO THE MOVERS AND SHAKERS OF THE WORLD. TALK TO THE MOVED AND THE SHAKEN."

— PETER JENNINGS

"MOST NEUROSES AND SOME PSYCHOSES CAN BE TRACED TO THE UNNECESSARY AND UNHEALTHY HABIT OF DAILY WALLOWING IN THE TROUBLES AND SINS OF FIVE BILLION STRANGERS."

— ROBERT A. HEINLEIN
STRANGER IN A STRANGE LAND

"AND I AM SURE THAT I NEVER READ ANY MEMORABLE NEWS IN A NEWSPAPER. IF WE READ OF ONE MAN ROBBED, OR MURDERED, OR KILLED BY ACCIDENT, OR ONE HOUSE BURNED, OR ONE VESSEL WRECKED, OR ONE STEAMBOAT BLOWN UP, OR ONE COW RUN OVER ON THE WESTERN RAILROAD, OR ONE MAD DOG KILLED, OR ONE LOT OF GRASSHOPPERS IN THE WINTER — WE NEVER NEED READ OF ANOTHER."

— HENRY DAVID THOREAU
WALDEN

"IT'S NOT THE NEWS THAT MAKES THE NEWSPAPER, BUT THE NEWSPAPER THAT MAKES THE NEWS."

— UMBERTO ECO
NUMERO ZERO

"BY GIVING US THE OPINIONS OF THE UNEDUCATED, JOURNALISM KEEPS US IN TOUCH WITH THE IGNORANCE OF THE COMMUNITY."

— OSCAR WILDE

"WORKING AS A JOURNALIST IS EXACTLY LIKE BEING A WALLFLOWER AT AN ORGY."

— NORA EPHRON

"BUT THE TELEVISION NEWS CAMERAS COULDN'T GET ANYWHERE NEAR THE ACTION, SO THE COVERAGE MOSTLY CONSISTED OF JOURNALISTS INTERVIEWING EACH OTHER ABOUT HOW LITTLE THEY KNEW."

— NEAL STEPHENSON

SEVENEVES

"IN SOME RESPECT JOURNALISM RESEMBLED SCIENCE: THE BEST IDEAS WERE THE ONES THAT SURVIVED AND WERE STRENGTHENED BY INTELLIGENT OPPOSITION."

— IAN MCEWAN

AMSTERDAM

"A CULTURE'S ABILITY TO UNDERSTAND THE WORLD AND ITSELF IS CRITICAL TO ITS SURVIVAL. BUT TODAY WE ARE LED INTO THE ARENA OF PUBLIC DEBATE BY SEERS WHOSE MAIN GIFT IS THEIR ABILITY TO COMPEL PEOPLE TO CONTINUE TO WATCH THEM."

— GEORGE SAUNDERS
THE BRAINDEAD MEGAPHONE

"THERE'S A PARABLE HERE SOMEWHERE, ABOUT THE DIFFERENCE BETWEEN JOURNALISM AND HISTORY. WHAT MIGHT APPEAR TO BE 'THE STORY' IN THE PRESENT MOMENT MAY ACTUALLY BE A DISTRACTION FROM IT, A SHINY OBJECT PREVENTING US FROM SEEING THE TRUTH OF WHAT IS REALLY GOING ON BENEATH THE SURFACE OF OUR ATTENTION, WHAT WILL MOST DEEPLY AFFECT PEOPLE'S LIVES IN TIME."

— MICHAEL POLLAN

THIS IS YOUR MIND ON PLANTS

"TO LOOK AT THE PAPER IS TO RAISE A SEASHELL TO ONE'S EAR AND TO BE OVERWHELMED BY THE ROAR OF HUMANITY."

— ALAIN DE BOTTON
THE PLEASURES AND SORROWS OF WORK

"PEOPLE DON'T ACTUALLY READ NEWSPAPERS. THEY STEP INTO THEM EVERY MORNING LIKE A HOT BATH."

— MARSHALL MCLUHAN

"EVERYBODY IS WRONG ABOUT EVERYTHING, JUST ABOUT ALL THE TIME."

— CHUCK KLOSTERMAN

SEX, DRUGS, AND COCOA PUFFS: A LOW CULTURE MANIFESTO

"I REALLY BELIEVE THAT THE MORE IDEALISTIC YOUR MISSION, THE MORE CUNNING YOU HAVE TO EMPLOY TO GET PEOPLE TO ENGAGE WITH WHAT YOU HAVE TO SAY."

— IRA GLASS

"OBJECTIVITY DOES NOT EXIST. THE WORD IS A HYPOCRISY WHICH IS SUSTAINED BY THE LIE THAT THE TRUTH STAYS IN THE MIDDLE. NO, SIR: SOMETIMES TRUTH STAYS ON ONE SIDE ONLY."

— ORIANA FALLACI

"I HAVE BEEN ASKING IF I'M AN ACTIVIST OR A JOURNALIST. AND MY ANSWER IS VERY SIMPLE. I'M JUST A JOURNALIST WHO ASKS QUESTIONS."

— JORGE RAMOS

"... IN A DEMOCRACY IT IS IMPORTANT THAT PEOPLE NOT ONLY SHOULD KNOW BUT SHOULD UNDERSTAND, AND IT IS THE ANALYST'S FUNCTION TO HELP THE LISTENER TO UNDERSTAND, TO WEIGH, AND TO JUDGE, BUT NOT TO DO THE JUDGING FOR HIM."

— ED KLAUBER

"WHENEVER THE MEDIA DO TRY TO PICK IT UP, IT SLIDES LIKE A LONE NOODLE FROM THEIR CHOPSTICKS."

— WILLIAM GIBSON
PATTERN RECOGNITION

"SUNLIGHT IS THE BEST DISINFECTANT."

— LOUIS BRANDEIS

"THE WHOLE IDEA OF TELEVISION NEWS OR ANY KIND OF NEWS IS TO INFORM PEOPLE ABOUT THINGS THEY NEED TO KNOW ABOUT."

— TED TURNER

"JOURNALISM IS WHAT WE NEED TO MAKE DEMOCRACY WORK."

— WALTER CRONKITE

"INDEPENDENCE OF THE MEDIA, FREEDOM OF THE PRESS, FREEDOM OF EXPRESSION AND THE RIGHT OF ACCESS TO INFORMATION ARE VITAL IF THE MEDIA ARE TO BE ABLE TO PERFORM THEIR WATCHDOG FUNCTION IN A DEMOCRATIC SOCIETY GOVERNED BY THE RULE OF LAW."

— OSCAR AULIQ-ICE

"SIMPLIFY, THEN EXAGGERATE."

— GEOFFREY CROWTHER

"I LIVED IN THE MIDDLE EAST FOR A LONG TIME, AND THE ONE THING I LEARNED AFTER LIVING THERE WAS THAT THERE IS NO ONE ABSOLUTELY ESSENTIAL TRUTH FOR ALL PEOPLE, AND THAT EVERY TIME I LOOK AT A COIN, I INSTINCTIVELY WANT TO LOOK AT THE OTHER SIDE."

— PETER JENNINGS

"WHEN A POPULATION BECOMES DISTRACTED BY TRIVIA, WHEN CULTURAL LIFE IS REDEFINED AS A PERPETUAL ROUND OF ENTERTAINMENTS, WHEN SERIOUS PUBLIC CONVERSATION BECOMES A FORM OF BABY-TALK, WHEN, IN SHORT, A PEOPLE BECOME AN AUDIENCE, AND THEIR PUBLIC BUSINESS A VAUDEVILLE ACT, THEN A NATION FINDS ITSELF AT RISK; CULTURE-DEATH IS A CLEAR POSSIBILITY."

— NEIL POSTMAN

AMUSING OURSELVES TO DEATH: PUBLIC DISCOURSE IN THE AGE OF SHOW BUSINESS

"THE NEWSPAPER IS A GREATER TREASURE TO THE PEOPLE THAN UNCOUNTED MILLIONS OF GOLD."

— HENRY WARD BEECHER

"EVERY TIME A NEWSPAPER DIES, EVEN A BAD ONE, THE COUNTRY MOVES A LITTLE CLOSER TO AUTHORITARIANISM."

— RICHARD KLUGER

THE PAPER: THE LIFE AND DEATH OF THE NEW YORK HERALD TRIBUNE

"THERE IS NOTHING TO FEAR EXCEPT THE PERSISTENT REFUSAL TO FIND OUT THE TRUTH."

— DOROTHY THOMPSON

"THE WAY TO RIGHT WRONGS IS TO TURN THE LIGHT OF TRUTH UPON THEM."

— IDA B. WELLS

ABOUT THE AUTHOR

Kit is a reader, writer, listener, and watcher of the human condition. He is the author of the IN 52 QUOTES book series.